Building Wiser Democracies

An International Active Citizenship Project

Ann Miller

Building Wiser Democracies -
An International Active Citizenship Project

Copyright © 2015 by Ann Miller

This book is dedicated to people everywhere who are willing to work together in partnership to heal and unite our divided world and to create a kinder and more peaceful future for everyone.

"Each of us literally chooses, by his way of attending to things, what sort of Universe he shall appear to himself to inhabit."
William James

"To cultivate kindness is a valuable part of the business of life."
Samuel Johnston

CONTENTS

INTRODUCING THE PROJECT

The Creative Learning Series

INTRODUCING THE PROJECT

If you think that Democracy needs a new direction, this project may be for you. As democracies throughout the world are struggling to reconcile social, economic and ecological tensions, this International Active Citizenship Project invites you to find partners to change the Democracy Script from the exclusively economic, to a more human-scaled and accessible script of personal, socio-economic and environmental wellbeing.

Just as the democracy movements of the eighteenth century focused on three ideas, Freedom, Equality and Justice, we can rethink Democracy for the twenty-first century by focusing on a *New Democracy Trifecta of People, Relationships and Infrastructure.*

Thinking of Democracy as an Ecological System rather than an Economic System enables us to deal with the complexity of Democracy in a more flexible and accessible way.

- Ecosystems have diverse species and complex processes, where actions occur at different levels, and at different speeds, sometimes interactively and systematically, sometimes independently and sometimes chaotically. An ecosystem contains many species and communities, as well as a physical environment.
- Democracies also contain many "species" of people, and many communities, all of which are in relationship with each other and with the natural and man-made environment.

It helps to focus our energies for progress if we think of the Democracy Script as a *New Democracy Trifecta.*

The New Democracy Trifecta.

1. People

Individuals are important in wise democracies. Everyone counts as part of our Global Human Potential, and we progress by nurturing the potential of each person and by providing good healthcare, good education and good work. The individual in a democratic society expects to be respected as an equal, and to be rewarded for good work, creativity and innovation. Social Justice and Social Inclusion are strong aspects of wise democracies which value individuals and put the fundamental Human Rights of freedom from fear and want at their core.

2. Relationships

Relationships are important in wise democracies. Our Socio-Economic relationships are what help us to maximize our Human Potential, and wise democracies ensure that strong social and economic relationships are forged between all sections of society. Harnessing human potential means valuing our individual and collective knowledge, training and experience, which provides an advantage for human progress. A balanced approach to job creation, spending and taxation creates a successful society where every person is included in the success.

3. Infrastructure

Infrastructure is important in wise democracies. Wise democratic governments develop systems, policies and procedures which allow people to function optimally and flourish. The infrastructure of a democratic society includes a wise consideration of Environmental Sustainability, not only locally but also globally. The resources of our Earth are our precious common inheritance and wise stewardship is our joint responsibility. Within states, controlling partisanship is a necessity for this continuous work to be accomplished even with changing governments.

Why Rethink the Script?

The Capitalist Democracy model which has been pursued since 1945 has now run its course. Reconstructing post-war economies and fostering growth was seen as the priority after WWII, and international competition helped achieve that goal, spurring citizens on to greater effort. Consolidating Capitalist Democracy was also seen as a bulwark against Communist Dictatorship, which was seen as a carry-over from pre-1945 totalitarianism.

The world today, seventy years on, is a vastly different place, and we need to find a new way to think about what we want our democracies to be, and how we will achieve that goal. We have all evolved and our social, economic and environmental knowledge and understanding have evolved as well.

To put what we have learned into practice requires that we change how we frame our idea of Democracy, and that is what this project invites you to do. Our intrinsic motivation to improve how we all live our lives is what we will harness here.

Human behaviour is an individual and collective choice, and choosing wisely depends on thinking carefully about the options and alternatives, and setting meaningful goals. When the activities of everyday life are invested with meaning, we are living with purpose and passion.

What better way could there be to live than to be engaged in a project whose end point is a better life for everyone? We can all participate in this project using our particular skills and experience, and finding partners to work with us. Progress comes from creating a space to allow new ideas to flourish, and success is more likely when meaningful shared goals are clearly understood by everyone.

The Creative Action Plan for this international project is simply stated:

Find partners to explore how we can re-define and re-energize our democracies using the *New Democracy Trifecta of People, Relationships and Infrastructure* as the framework. The aim of this project is to increase personal, socio-economic and environmental wellbeing to benefit everyone.

1. **People -** Personal wellbeing for every citizen.
2. **Relationships -** Socio-economic wellbeing for every society.
3. **Infrastructures -** Environmental wellbeing for the entire world.

Your engagement in this Active Citizenship project can provide a range of positive experiences and outcomes – social connectedness, challenge, enjoyment and the satisfaction of contributing to societal progress and creating a better future for everyone. A key dimension for this project is understanding and respecting the needs of all, and that intention can be well met by forming partnerships with divergent groups of people, so that a wide range of voices can be heard.

ONE

Rethinking the Democracy Script

This project is part of *The Creative Learning Series a Lifelong Learning Course in Personal and Social Development and Active Citizenship*, which aims to help you to grow and develop throughout your life. We are all creative lifelong learners because life itself is a continuous learning experience, where our experiences, ideas and dreams are stimulated personally, socially and professionally by all of our encounters.

I hope this project adds to your experiential learning, and that you will find satisfaction in making an active contribution to our global society by participating fully with others with the intention of making a difference.

Motivation is the key to all successful learning and our capabilities to learn are not only a consequence of innate intelligence but also our intention to learn something which is meaningful to us. Where we are is not where we have to be in our democratic development, and focusing on developing our social, economic and environmental intelligence in the context of advancing democracy offers a creative opportunity which does not depend entirely on what we have done up to now.

We have been running to stay where we are for some time now, and if we keep doing what we have been doing, we can't progress. We are caught in closed-loop thinking.

Breaking Out of the Closed Loop

This project offers the chance to break out of the closed loop and build our knowledge and experience by devising social, economic and environmental strategies for success.

Our multinational, global societies bring particular challenges, not least to Active Citizenship and Lifelong Learning. We "Learn Democracy" by doing it, but, like all learning, it helps if we have a direction and a purpose. You are in charge of your destiny when you take control and start to design your own "Curriculum for Democracy" and focus on the democratic values which are important to you. When selfish interests are what guide us, we are prone to forget about the equal rights and shared values which are at the root of the whole idea of Democracy.

The accumulation of wealth by the new elites of our global economy is not connected directly to the Nation State, but is global in its source. Unlike the successful citizens of the late twentieth century, where worker-consumers built wealth in national contexts, today's wealthy make and sell their goods and services globally. Their ongoing success is not directly linked to their fellow national citizens. In effect, they "owe them" little or nothing for their success.

The high-tech and financial services sectors are largely detached from individual states – they are stateless. Individuals are free to seek the cheapest way to make goods and profit, and they do. They see themselves as free economic agents in a global game and as deserving winners for taking the risks that they do. They feel no debt of obligation to society, and follow the selfish philosophy of Ayn Rand, which sees the rich as makers of fortunes, in contrast to the mass of citizens, who are takers of that wealth.

This script is not conducive to the give-and-take or the win-win required for social cohesiveness or world peace. As it continues, it escalates social unrest and results in an increase in state measures of social control.

To break this cycle we need to redraft the narrative, and we start by asking the question "Who writes the story of Democracy?" The answer is "We do – the collective citizens of the world."

To become fully Active Citizens, individuals need to take ownership of their democracies. A major purpose of Democracy is to encourage involvement and to enable individuals to have influence in the world through evolving understanding of themselves, their capabilities and their connections to others, by considering questions such as "How is power to be balanced between individuals and institutions in a democratic society?"

This project offers a means to explore questions about Democracy by joining together with others through social network sites and the power of the Internet. Social participation is what Democracy is all about, and the learning and knowledge creation that is achieved through participation in social networks has much to contribute to the development of Active and Informed Citizens.

We learn about Democracy by doing it, and we learn it best by doing it with others who share our passions and goals. By participating in collaborative deliberation and finding partners to act with us, we create influential communities of democratic actors to effect change. Democratic partnerships support individual learning, social development and participation in a real sense.

The Creative Learning Series takes the form of E-Books to facilitate maximum distribution of the ideas which are designed to serve your individual, social, environmental and political interests and outcomes. The series aims to support self-actualization and societal transformation. We learn how to live best by fully participating in life, by engaging with the world and by combining a focus on personal, social, economic and environmental priorities and issues. We open up the opportunity to creatively re-define Democracy for today's reality, and as we express ourselves this way, with others, we transform each other. The goal of Lifelong Learning is based on this understanding of shared cultural responsibility.

The benefits of working in partnership are many, but three stand out:

1. Engaging individual knowledge and experience
2. Encouraging active participation in shared goals
3. Acknowledging diversity and its value through teamwork

If we focus our energies on creating success in one of the three areas of *People, Relationships or Infrastructure*, leading to individual, socio-economic or environmental wellbeing, what would we have to change? As a group, make a decision about three specific actions you can implement to improve one of the three areas. Just by making this small contribution, you can make a difference. When we multiply the effect many times over, through all of the groups who participate, significant changes can happen.

TWO

Focusing Our Collective Energies

In 1990, a Creative Education Foundation survey identified the future skills requirements of the Fortune 500 list of the world's top companies. They identified the following as the top five – Teamwork, Problem-Solving, Interpersonal Skills, Oral Communication and Listening. These are skills we all need to be cultivating if we are going to create Wiser Democracies, and one of the fundamental decisions we need to make is whether we are going to focus on Capitalist Market-Making or Democracy for People.

The main objective of politicians at the moment seems to be to gain or retain power, prestige and profit, for themselves, their supporters and lastly, their societies, and these motives are entirely in line with those of business and industry. In elections, voters choose the party which will govern, and they are asked to choose between competing platforms.

How these platforms are constructed and presented is crucial to the outcome – who is elected and how they will behave in office. It is my belief that how we frame the goals of our democracies determines the Democracy we get, and that we advance Democracy best by deciding to share success, not just to compete, and by focusing our energies on a clear script which benefits the most people.

The G20 Summits have the stated objective of creating strong, sustainable and balanced economic growth. The collective action of the twenty most powerful states in the world is focused on ensuring that the benefits of prosperity are shared by all segments of society and on creating employment opportunities for more people. How successful are they in achieving that goal?

The members of the G20 are all from the world's largest advanced and emerging economies, representing about two-thirds of the world's population, 85 percent of global gross domestic product and over 75 percent of global trade.

The twenty permanent members are Argentina, Austria, Brazil, Canada, China, France, Germany, India, Indonesia, Italy, Japan, Republic of Korea, Mexico, Russia, Saudi Arabia, South Africa, Turkey, UK, USA and the European Union. The invited guests for 2015 are Spain (a permanent invitee), Malaysia, Zimbabwe, Senegal, Azerbaijan and Singapore.

The agenda for the November 2015 meeting rested on three pillars:

1. Strengthening the Global Recovery and Lifting the Potential – investment, employment and trade.
2. Enhancing Resilience – a healthy and stable financial system.
3. Buttressing Sustainability – development, energy and climate change.

Every wise leader understands the necessity of an "esprit de corps" – a spirit of common understanding and cooperation – in the attainment of success. This spirit of "harmony of purpose" is cultivated by creative and collaborative action planning, when a group of people works together to achieve collective and meaningful goals. However, if the goals are all skewed towards economic goals, the outcomes reflect that restricted concentration.

The story of strong profits and business investment, rising living standards and Keynesian welfare-state fine-tuning which defined the post-war golden age, when wages in the west doubled in a generation, is not the world of today. The west was still exploiting the resources of the less-developed countries in that post-colonial age.

If everyone in the world now were to consume the same as western citizens, the planet would probably only be able to sustain about one billion people, and at the moment, the whole world aspires to attain that level of wealth.

With a population of over seven billion and rising, talking about economic growth in the same old way is at best short sighted, at worst, suicidal. Yet our world leaders continue with their "business as usual" rhetoric of continuous growth.

Refocusing our energies and effort is an urgent requirement if we are to change how things are. The global democracy rankings for 2014 list the top twenty democracies, in order, as follows: Norway, Switzerland, Sweden, Finland, Denmark, Netherlands, New Zealand, Germany, Ireland, Belgium, Austria, Australia, United Kingdom, Canada, France, United States of America, Hong Kong, Spain, Portugal, Slovenia.

When we compare this list with the G20 countries, we notice that the top seven best democracies are not in the G20. Neither is Ireland, Belgium, Austria, Hong Kong, Portugal or Slovenia. Russia is 97th and China is 106th – neither is a democracy, but they are wealthy members of the G20.

Hungary is not a member of the G20, but the Hungarian president, Viktor Orban, was quoted in Bloomberg News in July 2014: *"The global financial crisis in 2008 showed that liberal democratic states can't remain globally competitive."* He listed Russia, China and Turkey as examples of *"successful nations, none of which is liberal and some of which aren't even democracies."* The question we are considering here is "What wealth is ethically justified, and what wealth is gained from exploitation of people and the environment?" All wealth is not equally ethically obtained.

Freedom House lists the *Political Rights and Civil Liberties* which are found in the best democracies as: Electoral Process, Political Pluralism and Participation, Function of Government, Freedom of Expression and Beliefs, Associational and Organizational Rights, Rule of Law and Personal Autonomy and Individual Rights. The best democracies are also identified by having free access to education, healthcare and employment, and the problems of maintaining the best democracies include political infighting, decreasing political participation, reduction in civil liberties and the domination of technocrats.

Having a wise democracy is not easy and requires citizen participation to keep up standards. Only 15% of the world's citizens enjoy the full fruits of democracy, 50% live under some sort of democracy, and 33% live in authoritarian regimes. There is work to be done if democracy is worth advancing as a system of government. Is the work worth the effort? How difficult would it be to make a difference? Democracy locates all of us as citizens who can change things if they need to be changed, and developing engaged citizens is the goal of this international partnership project *Building Wiser Democracies*.

Democratic governments pursue more social and economic reforms, they provide more schools and more public goods, and they negotiate with public unrest rather than squashing it by force. We're talking about the *quality* of human wellbeing rather than the *quantity* of wealth as money.

In any society, wealth brings influence, and cronyism is a potential problem. In a democracy, governments have to be accountable to too many voters for cronyism to have more than a manageable effect. Of course, cronyism exists, as it does everywhere, but the rich are outnumbered by the masses, and numbers count in this case. The influence of the rich can only have so much sway in any fair system of government. The institutions of government and society are a reflection of us, and political intelligence and political fluency only get better with practice. Your involvement counts.

THREE

Exploring Citizenship and Learning

The great government debates which have gone on since the 1970s about Active Citizenship and Lifelong Learning all revolve around concerns about productivity and competitiveness in the world economy, and to a lesser extent, social exclusion. Government policies see the development of individual skills and qualifications through Lifelong Learning as ways to address these issues, but the cause and effect relationship is far from simple.

Throughout the developed world, more and more young people are educated to diploma and degree level, and the result is that employers are demanding more and more qualifications, regardless of what is required to do the job. The profile of participation in further education is already skewed to the middle and upper classes of society, and this job-selection preference by employers only skews the advantages even further in the same direction. The introduction of formal accreditation and assessment for courses which were previously non-accredited or based on continuous learning serves to further limit accessibility and uptake, as do the rising costs of further education.

The focus on economic rather than personal and social rationales for further education and training marginalizes even more people. Factors like housing, health, income and family values, as well as the increasing costs of further education, all affect educational opportunities and uptake. A policy which places emphasis on skills and qualifications for economic competitiveness, and which puts the emphasis on individual responsibility for accessing and paying for formal education also misses the opportunities available through promoting learning which involves informal relationships of trust found in community-based policies to support social inclusion and cohesion. Each has a role to play in a balanced approach.

Creating partnerships between citizens with different perspectives provides a Learning Community which brings people to the table who have a range of knowledge and experience. What we need is a range of solutions which include *policies* focusing on structural provision, and *strategies* which empower individuals to enable them to make a difference. We are aiming to reconfigure the relationship between state, civil society and individual communities and citizens.

Building wiser democracies is the focus of this project, and that involves ensuring that policies are effective in providing opportunities for them to be developed. Democracy in action is multiple, contested and complex. There is no "easy fix" which is why Democracy and Lifelong Learning go together.

There are different approaches to how Democracy can be developed, the nature of the problems it is addressing and the extent to which Active Citizenship can influence change. There is no single recipe for Democracy. As a partner in this project, you will be developing strategies for effective Active Citizenship, by sharing knowledge and expertise as well as experiences of success and failure.

Resilience is a quality crucial to the process of Democracy Development. As citizens working together you will help each other through set-backs and learn how to do "policy work" of your own. Setting clear objectives is one way of focusing your energy on meaningful outcomes.

Throughout the world, democracies are struggling to come to terms with fundamental changes in the forces and factors of production, brought about by a shift from an industrial to a knowledge-based economy, and the opening up of previously under-developed areas of the world. Vast social, cultural and economic changes have been building up in the seventy years since WWII, propelled by global developments in technology, trade and manufacturing, agriculture and financial systems.

Add in aging populations, urbanization, increased migration, energy and environmental concerns, and worries about funding for welfare and pensions, and the pressures on Democracy are immense.

Change can open up opportunities for highly educated and skilled individuals, but this is not the case for poorly educated people and those who lack the necessary skills, either because of a lack of formal education, or the redundancy of existing knowledge and skills due to the changing workplace.

Lifelong Learning is increasingly important to help well-trained people be flexible and productive, and to upgrade the skills of the poorly trained, who face unstable employment, low wages or unemployment.

The world is changing, and our democracies need to change too. That means each of us needs to get involved in embracing personal and social development of all kinds, to make sure that any changes are wisely considered and implemented. We get the Democracy we deserve if we don't become Active Citizens for wise change.

In this International Partnership Project, we are learning by doing. As Active Citizens, we are *participating in the process* of becoming a member of a community of learners whose specialist subject is Democracy. We are learning about how to make our democracies work better. We are creating new knowledge and putting it into practice. We are engaging in improving our societies by applying what we learn from each other. None of us is an expert, but we can all help each other to get better.

FOUR

Building Wiser Democracies Together

Building Democracy is a collective process of creation, where we learn together how to build a better society by cultivating creative outcomes of relevance to our particular society.

In today's post-industrial world, we are most concerned with balancing priorities between personal, socio-economic and environmental pressures, and in particular with balancing wealth and wellbeing between "insiders" who enjoy all the benefits of society, and "outsiders" who don't. The great aims of humanity for justice and equality are harder to achieve when individual aims conflict with societal aims.

The collective and collaborative work which builds wise democracies creates the continuous transformations produced by often anonymous groups of people who share the values of personal, socio-economic and environmental wellbeing, and strive to make these values reality.

We are bringing Creativity, Compassion and Learning together when we advance Democracy towards Wisdom. Facing the human challenges of our world requires a complex dialectical process of production and reproduction. In wise democracies, we are constantly reworking reality to elevate lives, and to improve our own daily life, by creative effort.

Each small act can potentially become relevant to society at large and today, creativity is a tool for survival as we redesign our futures in the Global Village. To create culture, we materialize what we first imagine as an idea or ideal. *People, Relationships and Infrastructures* is just such an idea, a *New Democracy Trifecta* for today's complex world. In this project, we are trying to create partnerships across cultures to enable us to build wiser democracies which are able to be "translated" more globally.

Our goal-oriented actions, or Active Citizenship Intentions, engage and motivate us to transform our societies. When we have clearly defined our intentions, we are able to focus our energies on the shared objective. We are involved in "expansive" learning where we join forces to create something new, a new *paradigm for global democracy*.

Harnessing international civil society in a project like this offers the potential of the above collaborative process to create a better world. Globalization is opening up new forms of political activity and civic engagement, particularly as Virtual Networks. Active Citizenship is no longer limited to individual nation states and national citizenship.

Democratic Citizenship involves rights and responsibilities, empowerment and participation, whatever the cultural setting. Civil and Political rights include freedom of speech, religion and assembly, and the rights to petition the government, vote and receive due process with the legal system.

This is particularly challenging in traditional societies, where religious leaders dominate political discourses. Social and Economic rights are less challenging to these societies - rights to education, health care, a basic living wage, safe working conditions, unemployment insurance and retirement pensions.

Supporting social and economic rights through public taxes, regulation and the redistribution of wealth is a source of controversy in many societies, although Human Rights are seen as being held legitimately by all human persons, regardless of one's national citizenship. As stated in the American Declaration of Independence:

"We hold these truths to be self-evident, that all men are created equal, that they are endowed by their Creator with certain unalienable Rights, that among these are Life, Liberty and the pursuit of Happiness. That to secure these rights, governments are instituted among Men, deriving their just powers from the consent of the governed."

The liberal model of democratic citizenship is tied to the principles of Universal Equality and Popular Sovereignty: *"Government of the people, by the people and for the people"* is how Democracy should work, as Abraham Lincoln expressed it.

In the USA, the "rights" of the Declaration and the Bill of Rights remained closed to women, slaves, aboriginal peoples, immigrants and native born white men not holding private property for many years after the signing of the Declaration. Democracy is an evolving principal, even today, in the USA and throughout the world.

The attainment of today's democratic models of citizenship have arisen from many generations of motivated and responsible citizens being willing to invest the time, energy and resources to work to improve the Public Good. Today's global citizens hold international institutions as well as national governments accountable for upholding principles of justice, equality and transparency.

To be fully human is to be politically active. Today's rights were hard won by social movements in the past, and there is no room for free-loaders or complacency. Democratic freedoms were so important that people died for speaking out against social injustices, and even today, full participation is a far-off dream for many citizens of the world.

"Personal power, properly understood, is nothing but the ability to achieve purpose…What is needed is a realization that power without love is reckless and abusive, and love without power is sentimental and anaemic."
Dr Martin Luther King Jr

Through developing your personal power, you can share your valuable gifts with the world, and it is your duty to do so. Each of us gets to choose the role we wish to play and to write our part in the script which we create together. Democracy is an exercise in improvisation.

The Victory of Democracy in Europe on 8th May 1945 is celebrated as VE Day all over the world, and rightly so. The defeat of Nazism was a momentous event in the history of Democracy. Germany today is a fierce protector of Democracy because of the experience of Totalitarianism. World War Three is unthinkable, and the European Union's function is as much to defend and extend Democracy and Peace as to increase the wealth of individual states.

A mature and wise democracy is able to understand the need to constantly reconcile individual and group interests. This process is never a "once-and-done" exercise.

Democracy is also a struggle for equal rights by the outsiders of society, which involves intellectual, legal and grassroots activists aiming to launch new ways of thinking about inclusion, citizenship, and rights and responsibilities. They represent the marginalized in our societies and Democracy legitimises their right to demand better as their share of freedom and opportunity.

To change long-held assumptions of prerogatives and power, long negotiation is required, and the courage to press forward. All that is asked for is an equal chance in the field of potential and endeavour. In wise democracies, we all realise that we are creating new collective persona and meanings, based on putting people first.

The *New Democracy Trifecta of People, Relationships and Infrastructure* enables us to keep our focus on the end-game as we build and grow together.

We understand that we are all subject to selfishness, prejudice and stereotyping and that freedom of speech gives everyone the right to challenge the government of the day, who are citizens like us. Government policies are there to ensure equity and social justice, and if they fail to achieve that goal, they must be revised.

The strength of Democracy is vested in this requirement for government to be accountable to the citizens. Democracy is politically constructed, and we all have a part to play in that construction, determining the political, social, cultural and economic conditions of our communities.

FIVE

Using Commons and Power Wisely

The term "commons" is derived from British social history, where *The Commons* was the common land held by the whole village, and used for grazing livestock. The principle of free access to commonly held goods depended on a fair-use policy, adhered to by everyone.

The Thing was the name given to the governing assembly of Celtic society, which was made up of the free people of the community, who met in a place called *The Thingstead*, often held on the Common, under a prominent tree. There, the community reached decisions through discussion, presided over by law-speakers, so the Thing was a forerunner of the modern Parliament, a form of early Democracy.

Today, the term lives on in the national legislatures and political and judicial institutions of Northern European countries, particularly in the Isle of Man parliament, the Tynwald, and in the English term husting. Dingwall in the Scottish Highlands and Tinwald in Dumfries and Galloway are also derived from The Thing.

The *folkmoot*, or folk meeting, was the general assembly of the people of an area who reached decisions through discussion, a forerunner of the modern parliament, where disputes were resolved and decisions taken. The law-speaker or judge presided over The Thing to pass laws, elect leaders and judge according to the law.

Today, *Public Goods* include things like fresh water and air, as well as knowledge, and *Social Goods* are those provided by public funds (taxes) and delivered by governments through *Social Policy*. The *Public Good* is the common good or public interest, shared benefits at a societal level. *Common Goods* owned by sovereign states on behalf of the people include timber, coal, and fish stocks. All of these can be the subject of disputes within a society and between different states.

Global Commons are part of the heritage of humankind, and the responsibility of all of us to protect. Our progress and wellbeing as an entire species depends on us protecting our environment and ecology, and the Climate Change and Sustainable Resources discussions at global levels of government are an example of this world-wide responsibility. Global Public Health, Financial Stability and Knowledge Sharing are areas where international cooperation is crucial to our shared wellbeing.

These responses arise as shared responsibilities, determined by collective human actions, and the actions of individual citizens have a global impact. The Earth's shared natural resources are finite, and areas like the atmosphere, the deep oceans, Antarctica and Outer Space face problems of overuse or degradation because we are all able to use them. It is for this reason that representatives of world powers meet on a regular basis to discuss their shared responsibilities for Wise Stewardship of the Earth's resources.

Only by working together harmoniously in cooperation can we achieve sustainable success for ourselves. The urgency today is because of the rising population of the Earth. In the ancient times of *The Commons,* the Earth's total population was less than one million people – there was not the same urgency to collaborate beyond the local area. Then, as now, people understood that lasting success in any venture arises from an organized, shared knowledge expressed through planned collaborative action.

Three of the enemies of individual success are Poverty, Ignorance and Illiteracy, but the biggest obstacle to national and international success is Greed. When wealthy, successful people and states keep all of their wealth for their own good, instead of sharing their success for the good of all, we arrive at the position we are in today, where the gap between rich and poor is widening and social unrest increasing.

Life itself is organized energy, and learning how to harness this energy and put it to good use is what *The Golden Rule* is all about. Treating everyone with the same respect as you expect to receive from them is the challenge. Setting a goal and a purpose for your life, without violating the rights of others in the process, is the key to a healthy democracy and a life of ethical success.

"An aim in life is the only fortune worth finding."
Robert Louis Stevenson

A *Great Power* is a sovereign state that is recognized as having the ability to exert its influence on a global scale. Great Powers possess military and economic strength, as well as diplomatic and soft power influence, which may cause middle or small powers to consider their opinions before taking action on their own. There are three characteristics of great power status:

1. Power capabilities
2. Spatial aspects
3. Status dimensions.

The first G6 summit took place in France in 1975, and involved France, West Germany, Italy, Japan, the UK and the USA. In 1976, Canada was added, in1980, the European Union, and in 1998, Russia, making the G8, composed of the wealthiest developed countries on earth by national net wealth or by GDP, and the European Union, as a powerful confederation. Collectively in 2012 the G8 nations composed over 50 percent of global nominal GDP, the value of all final goods and services produced within a state in a given year using PPP – purchasing power parity.

The G8 countries meet regularly. There is an annual summit of G8 heads of government and the finance ministers, foreign ministers and environment ministers meet four times each year. The G20, the richest 19 individual countries and the European Union first met at the Washington Summit in 2008, following the global financial crisis, with a remit of discussing policy issues relating to the promotion of international financial stability. Between them, the G20 held 85% of gross world product, 75% of world trade and 66% of the world population in 2014.

The approximate GDP of the top ten is as follows:
1 European Union 19000 (billions of US$) 2 China 18000 3 USA 17000 4 India 7000
5 Japan 5000 6 Germany 4000 7 Russia 4000 8 Brazil 3000 9 France 3000 10 UK 3000

Compare that list with the 2014 Human Development Report Rankings:

1 Norway 2 Australia 3 Switzerland 4 Netherlands 5 USA 6 Germany 7 New Zealand 8 Canada 9 Singapore 10 Denmark 11 Ireland 12 Sweden 13 Iceland 14 UK

Wealth is not everything in the project of Wise Human Development.

SIX

Harnessing the New Democracy Trifecta

Prosperity is the guardian of democracy and peace, but human progress is not all about economic wealth. The *New Democracy Trifecta of People, Relationships and Infrastructure* provides a framework which helps us to focus our efforts on supporting people, supporting fair socio-economic relationships and supporting strong infrastructures and environmental sustainability, and offers us a way to harness our democratic potential on a global scale.

Supporting People – Human Development Potential

In a wise democracy, individuals are important. The individual in a democratic society expects to be respected and creativity and innovation are rewarded. Harnessing human potential means valuing our individual and collective knowledge, training and experience which provide an advantage for global human progress. Providing access to education, healthcare and welfare services maximizes opportunities and potential.

Supporting Relationships – Socio-Economic Potential

Supporting strong socio-economic relationships means providing real opportunities for everyone to contribute to society through meaningful work and fair wages. Public projects are one way of ensuring that every citizen has the dignity of participating in their community and gaining the ability to become an Active and Equal Citizen.

Supporting Infrastructure – Human Survival Potential

Providing and supporting a strong infrastructure is the crucial dimension of good governance. Enacting policies and procedures which support processes which allow people to function optimally and flourish is the specific work of government, and the global dimension of this work is imperative if our environment and ecology is to be protected and sustainable for the future.

Working Together as Partners

This international project invites you to find partners to work towards a solution which focuses our attention on the *New Democracy Trifecta of People, Relationships and Infrastructure*. Focusing on Education and Welfare, Inclusion and Respect, and Effective Policies and Procedures all enable us to harness human potential and resources in a sustainable way for the good of all. For any society, maximizing the potential of its people is crucial for progress.

Fostering social, economic and ecological intelligence is one way of thinking about the dilemmas was face. Creating international partnerships offers us all a way to step out of our individual nation state and its particular concerns and focus on ways of re-imagining Democracy, without the constriction of a purely economic lens, which serves to perpetuate global competition between nations.

Involvement in the international capitalist free-trade system has increased prosperity for some, but the balance needs to be reconfigured to enable more people to enjoy the fruits of that success. Poverty and frustration can only result in more civil unrest.

Is there a way to enable governments to change the script, and have the needs of ordinary people take centre stage, instead of responding mostly to the influential and already privileged?

The potential of a relevant project to empower people across the domains of their lives is what I am exploring here.

The shared knowledge approach, based on respectful relationships between non-partisan partners, aims to provide a participant driven and politically empowering forum for the exchange of ideas.

The kinds of resources, restrictions and life chances which people have access to and how they are distributed is what we are concerned with here. The valuable resources such as status, wealth, power and honour which define our position in the social structure give us the opportunity to help others gain the basic requirements of a dignified life. In doing this, we are creating a society where individual, socio-economic and environmental wellbeing are signifiers of political and democratic equality.

If only money and economic position determine influence and access to government, as it presently does, the Democratic Ideal of the Good Life is too narrowly allocated. Access to Education determines income and occupation, and integration into the labour market determines income, self reliance and social contacts. The drive to sustain middle and upper class lives in consumer societies supports the rise of global corporations and global capitalist expansion, often with military force. The capture of government by powerful financial interests, and the absolute power of the markets is where we are now, but it doesn't have to be that way.

The State, representing the People, has a significant role to play in re-balancing the democratic priorities to put people first, all people, not just the privileged few. Ensuring a dignified life for every citizen is at the centre of the social contract which is Democracy.

At present, democracies throughout the world share a dramatic disconnect between public communication and political decision making, where the activity of officials disregards public opinion. We need to somehow rebuild the political infrastructure of Democracy so that public authority can govern in the public interest.

Blaming inept politicians or greedy bankers and corporations ignores the fact that we are all citizens.

We can reconfigure our idea of Democracy without apportioning blame if we focus on creating a balance between social, economic and environmental priorities, and on creating a political infrastructure which enables us to address the issues openly.

Rethinking the primary rules and values of the political community and its members by engaging everyone in Active Citizenship would address the strain between representative and participative democracy.

SEVEN

Accepting the Responsibilities of Citizenship

In a Democracy, citizens are not clients or spectators in politics, although the current response to the global social and economic situation seems to be driven by elite professional politicians and economists. Democracy is predicated on the involvement of citizens in decision making, and democratic politics involves cooperation, consultation, consensus and challenge.

Open Democratic Politics takes place not only in the formal political forum but also in alternative, informal places. Democracy is about choices and careful consideration of competing options, with a view to serving the Common Good, yet reducing the whole of democratic politics to a quest for financial stability, performed mostly behind closed doors, reduces the potential for change.

The "unique solution" of austerity has significant negative effect on the already disempowered, those who have no resources to weather the storm, while the elites who were responsible for the current crisis go unchallenged and unaffected materially.

Conflict is a necessary part of Democracy, embedded in free speech – the right to challenge policies which adversely affect people. Complex and confident political systems accept positive and negative feedback from which they learn by adapting and changing.

Wise Democracy is a continuous feedback learning loop, involving public dialogue, civic engagement and compromise. Any challenge to the dominant government position can be seen as "acceptable" or "unacceptable" to the official participation process.

The Global Political Economy is under assault by forces who seek to empower and enrich themselves without contributing to the Common Good.

- At one end of the spectrum are the overtly criminal groups – drug cartels, human traffickers, arms dealers, computer hackers, and terrorists – who exploit loopholes of government.
- At the other end are the elites of every society who try everything to avoid the traditional obligations and responsibilities of citizenship – tax haven lawyers, currency speculators, industrial and mineral moguls – the new global super-rich have a vast army of allies who help them to evade taxation and exploit opportunities for profit.

Social, economic and environmental reforms are the last thing on their minds. The "state legacy" goods of social welfare – health, education and infrastructure – are under threat, but these mega-rich players seek only freedom of economic action to enrich themselves.

The social modernist era, from 1945 – 1970, saw the rise of the middle classes, who were encouraged and nurtured by their states to work hard, with the promise of an improved standard of living, and a welfare system to provide the cushion of social security. These post-war states were "welfare states" in the sense that they aimed to provide for the general welfare of the working classes, and to protect and lift up the poor by providing access to health and education services.

Healthcare, schools and pensions were collectively enjoyed "Public Goods". Elites felt a moral and ethical duty to contribute as successful citizens to the uplifting of the state, and during this period, the inequality of income gradually decreased. Democracy was advanced by the sharing of success, and in particular, by the sharing of economic gains between labour and capital.

From the 1970s, however, a shift occurred, as Individualism was promoted, and nation states focussed on maximizing opportunities for individual wealth accumulation instead of providing for the general welfare of a more equal society. This accelerated with the collapse of Communism in 1989. The civic-minded concept of development as the responsibility of the state and economic elites which was shared by communists and liberals alike, gave way to a laissez-faire race for wealth, by individuals and states alike. Greed became king.

The relationship between state and civil society was defined in a purely economic sense, and profit ruled the socio-political-economic climate. Collective social wellbeing was well down the list in the politics of Margaret Thatcher's UK and Ronald Reagan's USA, which involved the privatization of national industrial assets and deregulation of financial organizations. The rule of the technocrats which followed has brought us to the ideological crisis we are now facing, where the middle classes are squeezed by the global financial elite who seek to reduce the social services that are paid for by taxes, which they increasingly resent as illegitimate.

The ideological crumbling of the social modernist state is paralleled by the rise of this new class of global economic elites, enriched by opportunities created by deregulation. Unchecked corporate capitalism and the rise of authoritarian leadership in government go hand-in-hand with the mood of authoritarian workplaces, with their command- and-control managers.

Turning Passive into Active

Building Wiser Democracies is a grass-roots capacity building project which aims to help turn Passive Citizens into Active Citizens who understand that they are responsible for more than just fulfilling their duties of paying taxes and voting.

Active Citizens are free and equal to government officials who are elected by them, and together, they are supposed to work actively to change social injustices. It is important for all citizens to work together and participate in searching for solutions to public problems – poverty, exclusion and social inequalities.

Reducing Consumption

We also need to decide collectively how we can reduce the amount of "stuff" we currently use.

Our planet has limited resources to sustain our growing population, and we need to limit our use of them radically in order to restore our planet to a healthy state. For the Earth's ecosystem, which includes us, to thrive we need to ensure positive levels of health and resilience for everything and everyone.

This challenges our whole consumer mentality, and requires a paradigm shift in how we do things. Our use of the Commons, which is the whole of the Earth, has, up to now, largely ignored the cost of consuming Nature's dwindling resources. Nature needs us to work in harmony with it to restore the air, water and land to a healthy balanced state.

People invest time and energy in whatever issues seem most relevant to their social lives and governments respond, or choose not to respond, to what citizens bring to their attention. Social actions arise naturally from social existence and experience, and people who engage are performing Citizenship. They are Active Citizens with values, principles and priorities.

Human agency is the ability to control our moral conduct and to act ethically. Selective moral disengagement is when we ignore what is wrong by mentally restructuring it. For instance, we can blame people for their poverty when it is the work of governments to create the circumstance where opportunities for advancement and meaningful work can exist.

Forms of Influence

Active Citizens can use various forms of influence to galvanise world-wide support for Social Justice Issues which help us all to create a kinder, fairer world.

The small not-for profit groups working world-wide for social justice and ecological improvements number more than a million. Larger organizations like IDEA, the Institute for Democratic and Electoral Assistance, based in Stockholm, Sweden, involve governments, professional politicians, non-government organizations (NGOs) and individual citizens in their work.

IDEA is an intergovernmental organization with a mission to support sustainable democracy worldwide, by sharing comparative knowledge and experience in support of Democracy. The member states are Australia, Belgium, Canada, Finland, Germany, Netherlands, Norway, Portugal, Spain, Sweden and Switzerland, and their goal is to foster accountability in the equitable delivery of Public Goods – to ensure that public goods are delivered according to people's priorities rather than being hijacked for private interests. The IDEA pamphlet for their Democracy and Development Programme states:

"More substantive democracy requires mutual, active engagement from both political actors and groups of citizens in the daily functioning of the state in between elections: in making public policies address public needs, in providing services to the public in an effective way, in giving feedback for adequate reforms."

Your involvement in this project, *Building Wiser Democracies*, is your opportunity to get involved in driving reform agendas and improving the democratic accountability processes. We, as citizens, are the drivers of change on a local, regional and international level. By working together as equals we can enhance the political will for change. This collaborative approach to building Democracy emphasizes diversity and the equal participation of women and men, and facilitates the exchange of knowledge across boundaries and borders.

Sharing Social Power

Active Citizenship is the sharing of social power among citizens. It is a learned skill which improves with practice, when groups of people work together to effectively create or resist change. Sharing Power is the concept most difficult to achieve in any group, whether company or country. Leaders are accustomed to lead by making most if not all of the decisions, and they have followers who follow their lead. Questioning our assumptions is a necessary part of progress in any venture, and questioning our democratic leaders' assumptions of what their leadership means is a big part of advancing democracy in a wiser direction. Too many of them are autocrats in democratic clothing!

All questioning energises Democracy, and stops complacency. Democracy has no final definition, but describes an ongoing process of social and political dialogue. If we don't ask, we probably won't get the democracy we want. If we don't participate, we get the democracy we deserve. We live in a world of complexity, uncertainty, instability and conflicting values. As individuals, we each seek to take control of our life by engaging with the world around us, and by setting goals. This project invites you to find partners and to work together to make a difference locally, nationally or internationally by focusing on the *New Democracy Trifecta of People, Relationships and Infrastructure*. Only when these three are considered together, and a balance sought, can we achieve lasting success.

EIGHT

Learning to Be – UNESCO 1972

"Not only is it desirable to prevent economic, intellectual and civic disparities from becoming more acute, in the radically changing modern world, and to see a certain level of welfare, education and democracy become accessible to all peoples; it is something which we can no longer regard merely as a matter of philanthropy, charity, benevolence or loftiness of spirit…

So far as the economy, welfare and standards of living are concerned people no longer resign themselves so easily to inequality, dividing class from class, or to frustration afflicting whole nations, as in the days when it was seen as an arrangement of the Almighty of the natural order of things…

Finally, democracy itself has become a more impressive problem than ever. For, on the one hand, the peoples now aspire to democracy quite independently of their GNP, and their rates of school enrolment: but at the same time, they aspire to a different kind of democracy from the one to which we have until now been accustomed…"

The Faure Commission's Report for UNESCO stressed two fundamental ideas – the need for Lifelong Education and the need to create a Learning Society. In 1976, UNESCO published a report on Adult Education, where it stated:

"The term adult education denotes the entire body of organized education processes, whether the content, level and method, whether formal or otherwise…as well as apprenticeship, whereby persons regarded as adults by the society to which they belong develop their abilities, enrich their knowledge, improve their technical or professional qualifications, or turn them in another direction and bring about changes in their attitude or behaviour in the two-fold perspective of full personal development and participation in balanced and independent social, economic and cultural development."

Learning for Life

Wise democratic policies are informed by democratic "learning for life" which nurtures and cultivates the conditions for creative dialogue about what kind of societies we want to live in and how we can work together to build them. This involves tackling the significant problems in individual societies and involving citizens in solving them.

Political engagement in real issues which affect actual communities is rare. More typical is the politician's avoidance of contact with the actual public. Then there is "downloading", where governments abdicate responsibility for citizen welfare and the delivery of services previously paid for and provided by the state, leaving them to *"philanthropy, charity, benevolence or loftiness of spirit"* as the UNESCO report warned about.

Rather than accepting tokenism, Active Citizenship is about negotiating changes in society in an open manner, through communication and the pursuit of the Common Good. In a wise society, we recognise that we can't afford everything we might want, and we need realistic consideration of priorities, carried out in a transparent way.

In a positive circle, participatory democracy nurtures Civic Learning, and in turn this learning improves the quality of Active Citizenship. Active Citizenship is for everyone to practice, party leaders included.

Lifelong Learning and Active Citizenship

In today's world, it is increasingly important for us all to be Active Citizens, and to take responsibility for advancing Democracy and enabling more people to enjoy a dignified and fulfilling life. By sharing what we have learned, we can create a kinder, fairer world for our children to inherit. We can make a difference to how things are. We can create a win-win, where everyone gains.

Lifelong Learning is an imperative in our fast-changing world, and by examining how things came to be how they are, we can decide what we need to change to create a better world. Epistemology is the study of what we know and how we know it, and it enables us to understand that knowledge is not objective, but a social construct and part of a political system that creates culture.

As people in a particular culture agree upon the meanings that they give the world around them, they classify their experiences and encode them in order to think and talk about them. What we "know" is subject to what we believe, and what we believe depends on how we think about and conceptualize our experiences. Knowledge is not an accumulation of "facts" but an *interpretation* of our collective experiences.

This accounts for worldwide cultural differences about what constitutes knowledge. As Thomas Khun (1962) pointed out in his study of the development of knowledge, every society has a prevailing framework, or "paradigm", which remains uncritically accepted as true until a new paradigm replaces it.

When we think, we are embedded in a whole set of *assumptions* about what is true or legitimate, what is authority, what counts as evidence and who and what influences us. We need to be aware of our assumptions and challenge them when they no longer serve us.

We need to constantly question how we can create a better society or a better world, as our answers to these questions affect our definitions of ourselves, the way we interact with others, our public and private personae, our sense of control over life events, and our conceptions of right and wrong and social justice.

The elites in any society naturally seek to retain access to the positions, power and resources which give them privileges and dominance, and they also seek to influence how people in that society perceive success, and whether and how they can achieve it for themselves. In every society, patterns of discrimination against disadvantaged groups continue to exist, and these limit access for people who do not "fit in" with the ideas of the elite group of a particular society.

Gender, race, ethnicity, social class, age and income are all barriers to inclusion which still exist, even in advanced democracies, where equality of opportunity is held up as a necessary cornerstone of social justice in a fair society.

Education, Employment and Health issues have galvanized political consciousness globally, because they relate to how prevailing political systems reinforce and sustain power inequalities within a given class, race, age and gender group. These major social structures, Education, Employment and Health, provide an important way to reform societies.

Current definitions of health and wellbeing expand the definition to include the physical, emotional, social, intellectual and spiritual dimensions of a person's life. Exclusion from educational, employment and health-care opportunities has a significant effect on a person's total life experience, inextricably linked to his or her place in society.

By recognizing the particular obstacles which certain individuals face, we can work together to reform our systems and make them more responsive and inclusive. This paradigm shift can only happen when enough people are willing to recognize and speak out about the inequities which exist in the current system.

We advance democracy by sharing success, and only by improving how we are currently sharing access to the resources of education, employment and health-care can we effect real change in societies throughout the world, including our own. This is not a problem only for under-developed areas of the world – we can all do better.

The Creative Learning Series harnesses the power of human imagination or consciousness to create change - we generate an idea, we organize the elements which will enable us to proceed and then we develop the plan through direct action.

Democracy is just such an idea and its development is a continuous process of improvement. It will never be perfect, but it can always be improved, and each of us has a part to play in making that improvement.
Individuals can not only change the world, they have a duty to do so, and "*It does not have to be this way*" is the thought which drives the progress of human civilization. We each have a gift to enable us to contribute, and we are equally responsible for the outcome. We all have different ways of doing things, and we all have gifts which bring satisfaction to us, and which can be used to help others.

By being the best you can be, you help others to be the best they can be. By bringing your talents to the team and striving for continuous improvement, you are able to make the best use of your talents, and make your best contribution.

By being creative, you develop the skills of enterprise, imagination, curiosity, risk taking and courage, which enhance your capabilities and capacities. You develop an enthusiasm and a joie de vivre which will bring joy to you and which will be attractive and "infectious" to other people. Creativity is about growing and evolving, looking into things with an enquiring and open mind, and living a life of purpose and passion.

The fourteen books of *The Creative Learning Series* offer a range of strategies to help everyone to attain personal success and to create a better community, society or world. You are invited to join this social enterprise and collaborative initiative and find partners to work together with purpose and passion to make a difference in our world.

NINE

Practising Ethical Capitalism

Shared knowledge and collective action can make a significant difference in the world. The main aim of the Creative Learning Series is to serve as a catalyst for individuals and communities of people who care about the same issues to work together to effect changes. Active Citizens can use various forms of influence to galvanise world-wide support for ethical business practices. The citizen as consumer holds as yet untapped power to persuade businesses and governments throughout the world to institute changes to production practices to protect and heal the environment.

Promoting a greener, cleaner and more planet-friendly market place is what Ethical Capitalism is all about. The power of Citizen Consumers working together can make ethical choices the norm for businesses. When buyers care, companies care, and they then make smarter products and choose smarter processes. Not to do so is to lose business to competitors who make the necessary changes. The Carbon Footprint and Life-Cycle Cost Analysis give hard evidence of environmentally harmful processes.

Modern life, by its nature, carries risks, and the chemicals which fuel our life in affluent societies give rise to the diseases of civilization which are rare in less-developed societies. Endocrine disorders like diabetes and auto-immune disorders like asthma, multiple sclerosis and lupus result from the overproduction of free radicals in our bodies. When biological stress causes a reduction in antioxidants, chronic inflammation leads to the long-term medical conditions which are becoming all too common in modern societies. The costs of these are huge, to individuals and to the community at large, through increased medical costs and lost production.

Lead, mercury, diesel fuel and pesticides are among the culprits, but we all regularly consume a toxic cocktail of chemicals about which we are largely ignorant. Each of us has a different threshold and tolerance before the burden of chemicals overwhelms our system and we succumb to the chronic inflammation which is the root cause of the above conditions. Years of accumulation can seriously undermine the immune system and result in the diseases of the heart and lungs and various cancers.

When we travel about the world, we are subjecting our bodies to unknown risks. Much could be improved with a more transparent system such as the REACH (Registration Evaluation and Authorization of Chemicals) programmes run by the European Chemicals Agency, which started in 2009 to rigorously test all of the current chemicals in use, to enable manufacturers to find alternatives for those which can be improved upon.

The LEED Certification (Leadership in Energy and Environmental Design) which is part of the Green Building Movement aims to create ecological transparency and offer market ready alternatives to increase comfort, health, and cost savings. This is a good example of where producers and consumers can work together to produce changes which benefit everyone. The bar for these initiatives, as for Democracy, is one of continuous improvement, informed by social engagement. The search for sustainable resources is the key driver in the Green Building Movement.

Consumer Citizens play their part by rewarding producers who are environmentally sensitive and whose practices are socially and environmentally responsible. Health and Wellbeing are at the centre in this reciprocal system, which harnesses collective action to improve the environment and to improve living and working conditions.

Creating collective consumer action is a very powerful way to effect change in production methods by integrating social responsibility into a company's strategy for success.

Resetting the balance between poor producers and rich consumers can start with building awareness among elite consumers who are concerned about social issues like health and the environment.

Building a healthier world involves all of us being socially and environmentally responsible, and the rich nations have a duty to help the poorer regions to raise their game through better agricultural technologies, accessible education and fair wages and working conditions. Putting people's health before our desire for cheap goods is a challenge for consumers, but ethical purchasing is catching on.

Restorative practice and sustainability are high on the agenda in the Green Movement. Restorative practice means taking nothing from the Earth which cannot be replaced, regenerated or recycled, but governments, business and industry are the only institutions powerful enough to actually create change towards ecological and environmental sustainability, by legislating for ethical practices which involve treating every stage of production with a socially and environmentally sensitive approach and treating the whole world with respect.

This is a tall order for businesses whose main aim is profit, but businesses are run by citizens and citizens work in them. Learning how to redefine profit by thinking about the cost-benefit analysis of industrial practices is something we can all help with, either as advocates or as consumers. Business responds to its consumers as part of its normal practice, and our ethical responsibility as Active Citizens is to use our buying power to effect meaningful change in how we all do business.

If corporate interests trump everything else we can never turn the tide of global pollution. The Life-Cycle Cost Analysis of extractive industries like oil, mining and logging is a way to work out the true costs to citizens of this use of The Commons.

Private industries have previously been allowed to exploit the resources of the land and the costs have been passed on to citizens for adverse impacts to natural and infrastructure resources. Toxins released into rivers and landfills, polluted air and damage to roads have all been cleaned up using tax dollars from the Common Goods of society at large. This transfer of costs creates a strong ethical and fiscal incentive to find better ways of doing business.

Only governments can regulate businesses and industries and compel them to pay the full cost of their business as well as take full responsibility for damage to The Commons, but politicians often prefer not to confront their big funders. They also have a tendency to delay difficult decisions until they are out of office and in receipt of their political pension.

Citizen power is needed to persuade our elected politicians to do the right thing. By shining a light on what matters to you, you help others to join the cause. What businesses produce has to be balanced against what they deplete and damage, and environmental and social responsibilities are legitimate aspects of business costs in the modern world.

Citizens are also responsible for ensuring compliance, and holding the ethical line is up to all of us. Making a principled stand is easier when we work together with others. In a democracy, government is of the people and by the people, but it will only be *for the people* who are heard. It's up to all of us to make a stand and become Active Citizens, in charge of our own destiny and that of the Earth.

TEN

Becoming an Active Citizen

This international project offers an opportunity for everyone to become involved in *Building Wiser Democracies* at home and abroad. We can all help by making our contribution from where we are, and, by using our contacts, our skills and our resources, we can take action to make a difference. By working together in this way, we can make a difference to how life is for the many poor people in the world who see no hopeful future. We can share our good fortune and create a better world for all of us.

All people want the chance to earn enough to gain happiness and fulfillment, but social exclusion, disenfranchisement and marginalization manifest in poverty and crime, and ultimately result in social unrest as people react to social injustice. The solution needs partnerships between powerful and influential political, religious and economic organizations, and dynamic grassroots organizations.

The solution lies in making an active social, economic and political contribution which ultimately helps all of us live a better, richer life. Life is not about winning and losing – it's about how you play the game. Full humanity is achieved when you realize that your personal success is enhanced when you can share it with others. Being successful is about giving back and gifting forward, and we're here to make a difference and leave a legacy to the world. Helping others is a sign that you have been successful in understanding and playing the game, because you have enough for yourself and enough to share.

Democracy is a complex and difficult process, because in a Wise Democracy, government represents *all people*, not just the wealthy elites. When government exists to increase the wealth and power of its officials and the elite voters who keep them in office, democracy is being manipulated for another purpose.

The redistribution of wealth as income between rich and poor is the *pivot point*. The economic status quo is the instrument of change for any fairer system of wealth distribution, and the *ethos of choice* rests with the wealthy elites who hold the majority of the world's resources. These elites naturally seek to protect their own resources and wealth. It's human nature!

That's why we all need to be involved in the plan to create a fairer world. It is a challenge to move from a lip-service democracy to an actual system which looks out for the rights of all people to enjoy a dignified and fulfilling life. It is even harder if we project that goal on to a world stage. The competition between states is a very real impediment to addressing issues of poverty, because profit and wealth is the focus of the political elites who govern on our behalf.

Plutocracy, rule by the wealthy, and *oligarchy*, rule by a few dominant groups who pass their influence from one generation to the next, both result in "the politics of wealth-defense by materially endowed actors" as Jeffrey Winter observed in his 2011 book *"Oligarchy"*. Moving on from the market-driven capitalist democracies which predominate in the world, to a more equitable distribution of resources is a real challenge to all of us.

Building Wiser Democracies offers an opportunity for everyone to become involved in seeking solutions to this complex problem. Some of the best minds in the world are already involved, through the United Nations Development Agenda, in examining how national development strategies can enable peace, good governance and human rights. Social progress, social justice and social inclusion, through education and training, protection for children and promoting sustainable development, are all big issues which are daunting for ordinary citizens to comprehend.

We can all help, however, by making our contribution from where we are. We can use our contacts, our skills and our resources, and take action to make a difference. The will to action is the secret of life, and each of us can make a difference by changing things in small ways.

It seems daunting when we look round the world and see the pain and misery experienced by many millions of people on a daily basis, at home and abroad, but, living as we do in this world of extraordinary beauty, abundance and potential, we are each able to make a contribution to creating a better world, starting where we are:

Supporting Local Efforts

We can work together locally to support the basic needs of our own communities. By using your talents, contacts and initiative, you can make a real difference in the lives of your immediate neighbours, and in your wider community. Identify and nurture opportunities for positive change within communities, involving all stakeholders.

Participating in Global Initiatives

We all have ideas which can transform systems that keep people and countries at the margins of society and contribute to impoverishment. Working towards "enough for all" is a good place to start. We can learn from each other and benefit from mutual effort, mutual trust and mutual respect.

Promoting Full Employment

When people have work, they become stakeholders in society, not only economically. Employment and self-employment means dignity and self-determination, resulting in a positive psychological boost from contributing, which in turn affords a stable sense of identity and access to a social network. Living life to the full is about participating and contributing.

Promoting Inclusion

Supporting full participation in all aspects of social, economic and political life, including particularly the opportunity to work and access to appropriate education, information and support networks, gives people self-respect, which in turn leads to resilience in dealing with adversity.

We Need to Help People to Help Themselves.

Poverty, inequality and exclusion are three crucial determinants of social unrest. Poverty limits the access of people to the mechanisms of success and progress. As well as material deprivation, there is psychological disempowerment. Active Citizenship means making an active social contribution which ultimately helps all of us live a better, richer life.

Promoting Meaningful Change

If we do what we've always done, we'll have what we've always had. Roosevelt gave the United Nations its core aims – The Four Essential Freedoms of Democracy – freedom of speech and belief, and freedom from want and fear. is all about that. It's not that we don't know what has to be done to move forward, it's just that our current "democratic" system is over-whelmed by capitalist priorities, where people come second to profit, and we're all encouraged to overspend. Democracy

The New Democracy Trifecta gives us a framework for moving forward:

Prosperity is the guardian of democracy and peace, but human progress is not all about economic wealth. Focusing on the *New Democracy Trifecta of People, Relationships and Infrastructure* offers a way forward to revive Democracy for the twenty-first century. Supporting people, supporting fair socio-economic relationships and supporting strong infrastructures and environmental sustainability offers a way to harness our democratic potential on a global scale.

1. **People**

 Individuals are important in wise democracies. Everyone counts, and we progress by nurturing the potential of each person and by providing good healthcare, good education and good work. The individual in a democratic society expects to be respected as an equal, and to be rewarded for good work, creativity and innovation. Social Justice and Social Inclusion are strong aspects of wise democracies which value individuals and the fundamental Human Rights of freedom from fear and want which are at the core of our goal to create wiser democracies.

2. **Relationships**

Relationships are important in wise democracies. Good Socio-Economic relationships are what help us to maximize our potential, and wise democracies ensure that strong social and economic relationships are forged between all sections of society. Harnessing human potential means valuing our individual and collective knowledge, training and experience, which provides an advantage for human progress.

A balanced approach to job creation, spending and taxation creates a successful society where every person is included. Supporting strong socio-economic relationships means providing real opportunities for everyone to contribute to society through meaningful work and fair wages. Public projects are one way of ensuring that every citizen has the dignity of participating in their community and of gaining the opportunity to become an Active and Equal Citizen.

3. **Infrastructure**

Infrastructure is important in wise democracies. Providing and supporting a strong infrastructure is the crucial dimension of good governance. Enacting policies and procedures and supporting processes which allow people to function optimally and flourish is the specific work of government, and the global dimension of this work is imperative if our environment and ecology are to be protected and sustainable for the future.

The continued success of a democratic society requires consistent wise stewardship as our joint responsibility. Within nation states, controlling partisanship is a necessity for this continuous work to be accomplished even with changing governments.

The Importance of International Partnerships

Creating international partnerships offers us all a way to step out of our individual nation state and its particular concerns and focus on ways of re-imagining Democracy without the constriction of a purely economic lens, which serves to perpetuate global competition between nations. Involvement in the international capitalist free-trade system has increased prosperity for some, but the balance needs to be reconfigured to enable more people to enjoy the fruits of that success. Poverty and frustration can only result in more civil unrest.

By working in partnership, across borders and boundaries, we can change the policies and institutions which make the rich richer and the poor poorer at home and abroad. We can advocate for policies and support initiatives that respect the integrity of every human being, and offer the dignity of social inclusion to everyone, by supporting children, families and communities as they develop the capacities to solve their own problems.

We are the government and the government is us. Our collective actions can change our world.

THE CREATIVE LEARNING SERIES

The *Creative Learning Series* is designed to help you to develop your talents and explore your potential, improve your awareness and enhance your quality of life. By being creative, you develop the skills of enterprise, imagination, curiosity, risk taking and courage, which enhance your capabilities and capacities. You develop an enthusiasm and a joie de vivre which will bring joy to you and which will be inspiring to other people. Creativity is about growing and evolving, looking into things with an enquiring and open mind, and living a life of purpose and passion.

Here you will find plans, tools and techniques to support your personal development or that of your company, corporation or organization, and to increase our shared potential to make a difference in the wider community. In the modern world, it is increasingly necessary for each of us to have a way of looking at the big picture, and participating in the solutions to the world's problems, using our talents and our creativity to make a real difference.

The fourteen books and projects of *The Creative Learning Series* aim to inspire people everywhere to create a kinder world. You can learn to create your best life and our best world at the same time through *Creative Lifelong Learning* and *Creative Action Planning*. This social enterprise and collaborative initiative invites you to work together in partnership, using your particular skills and knowledge, to make things better for everyone. Each book in the series examines a different aspect of personal, social, professional and spiritual development, and invites you to participate by harnessing your *Creative Imagination*.

Creative Lifelong Learning is about fulfilling your own potential and also about working together to support things like advancing democracy, extending educational and employment opportunities, improving health, and alleviating poverty. It facilitates the exchange of experience and support through fellowship and partnership, as wise relationships are crucial in expanding the true understanding that we are all the same in our humanity.

Creative Action Planning harnesses the power of human imagination or consciousness to create meaningful and sustainable development - we generate an idea, we organize the elements which will enable us to proceed and then we develop the plan through direct action. Individuals transform the world by working together in partnership, and *"It does not have to be this way"* is the thought which drives the progress of human civilization.

We each have a gift to enable us to contribute, and we are equally responsible for the outcome. We all have different ways of doing things, and we all have gifts which bring satisfaction to us, and which can be used to help others. By being the best you can be, you help others to be the best they can be. By bringing your talents to the team and working together to improve things for everyone, you are able to make the best use of your talents, and make a contribution to the development of our shared Human Potential.

You are invited to join this global project and to encourage partners to work together with purpose and passion to make a difference in our world.

Book One – Creative Self-Development – Discover and Share Peace of Mind, Love of Life and Joy.

(Special Kindle Edition – Creative Self-Development – Creating the Unique Tapestry of Your Life)

Learn the art of creative self-development. Free your imagination and realize your full potential. Find out how your mind works, and how you can develop your consciousness over time to be all you can be.

Book Two – Life's Lessons – Working Together to Transform Education, Business and Government.

(Special Kindle Edition – Life's Lessons – Evolving Strong Democracy by Sharing Success)

Explore the development of Democracy throughout the world from 1776 to the present day, and consider how we can advance Democracy by sharing success and by transforming the key organizations of Education, Business and Government. By refocusing on our shared values and creating more inclusive societies, we can create a future worth living for our children and our children's children.

Book Three – Gifts from Yggdrasil – A Hero Quest for Today.

This interactive novel is your invitation to join the Hero Quest which is as old as humankind, and which is described in different ways by every culture, but always has the same aim – to create the best world we can imagine. If you are interested in venturing forth as a hero to find the answers to the problems of our world, this quest might be for you.

Book Four – Stress-Free Lifelong Learning – A Guide to Effective and Enjoyable Education for Everyone.

This International Project is designed for all Lifelong Learners, and whether you are a student, parent, educator leader or politician, this guide is designed for you. It offers strategies to enhance learning and teaching, and to encourage, inspire and connect individuals and organizations who want to help promote stress-free Lifelong Learning.

Book Five – Spirit's Gifts and Soul's Mission – A Course in Wise Relationships

By engaging in Wise Relationships, we can all transform our societies and our religions. This International Project invites you to become a partner and to join together with others to plan how we can bring reconciliation and peace to the religious strife which threatens the security and wellbeing of so many people throughout the world.

Book Six – At Peace with the World – A Little Book of Encouragement for Everyday Heroes

The twenty short stories in this book highlight everyday heroes who help ordinary people in their own communities by freely sharing their skills. These stories are designed to raise a smile, and raise your spirits. This book is for potential heroes and those everyday heroes who are already playing a part in making the world a better place, one person at a time.

Book Seven – Planning for Success – Going for the Win-Win in the Game of Life

By joining this International Project, you can explore all aspects of the successful life, and also work together with other people to maximise success for your community, organization or country. Planning is a process of choosing among the many options, and it is a skill which can be learned by practice. If you are failing to plan appropriately, you are wasting your energy and your time. Taking the time to undertake this project may be time well spent…

Book Eight – Building Wiser Democracies – An International Active Citizenship Project.

This International Active Citizenship Project invites you to find partners to change the Democracy Script from the exclusively economic, to a more human-scaled and accessible script of personal, socio-economic and environmental wellbeing. Just as the democratic movements of the eighteenth century focused on three ideals, Freedom, Equality and Justice, we can rethink democracy for the twenty-first century by focusing on a New Democracy Trifecta– People, Relationships and Infrastructure.

Book Nine – Harnessing the Pioneer Spirit - An Exploration of Possibilities and Potentials

This exploration of the Pioneer Spirit looks at all kinds of pioneers, past and present, and invites you to think about your own potential to explore new horizons. I hope you gain inspiration from this exploration of the Pioneer Spirit, just as I did.

Book Ten – Creating Our Best World – A Global Mindfulness Project

Mindfulness provides a win-win where you can find peace of mind and success for yourself and also help create a better world by working with partners on the project of your choice. The ABC of Mindfulness offers you a simple way to include Mindfulness in your daily life and the Mindfulness Script provides a method to work with partners worldwide to engage in positive change. Come and join us. You can make a difference.

Book Eleven - Choosing More Mindful Pathways - Living a Life of Purpose and Passion

This book is the sequel to *Creating Our Best Life – A Global Mindfulness Project*. It is designed to enable you to explore more ways you can include Mindfulness in your life and enjoy the advantages at home, at work and in the world. The decision to choose more mindful pathways is the first step on your journey to success.

Book Twelve - Building Pathways to Peace - Some Lessons in Mindfulness for World Leaders

The successful participants in this course will gain an increased potential to release new creative energy back into the world by solving the problems which are blocking our progress towards peace. Wherever conflict continues in the world, people suffer and poverty and pain proliferate. Mindful leadership is needed to move things on, and building pathways to peace is a way to begin the process of change.

Book Thirteen – The Creative Lifelong Learning Formula – Building Global Partnerships for a Sustainable World

The Creative Lifelong Learning Formula includes the key elements of *Creative Lifelong Learning* from the twelve books of *The Creative Learning Series*, as well as the tools and techniques for *Creative Action Planning*, which are currently only available as individual E-Learning projects. Here, you will discover how you can design your own Lifelong Learning pathway, create action plans to realize your potential, and become a partner in the *UN Global Strategy*. *The Creative Lifelong Learning Formula* offers a range of creative strategies and action plans to move the process along, and the *UN Global Goals* offer a comprehensive blueprint to focus your energies to help create a better world for all of us.

Book Fourteen – God and the Global Kindness Business – An Evolving Story of Partnership, Progress and Human Potential

What could be more important than creating a world of peace and plenty for all? *The Global Kindness Business* provides a way to join together with other partners and achieve the ultimate goal of world peace. This is a guide for partners who want to actively do the work of creating a kinder world, one step at a time.

In 100 steps, you can become inspired, informed and involved in *The Global Kindness Business* which has been helping people make progress since the beginning of time. Choose your pathway and your companions, and set out to change your life and our world. You won't regret it.

To become a partner in *The Global Kindness Business*, all you need to do is set out to try your best to make a difference. You can choose to make a difference locally, nationally or internationally, and wherever you start, your efforts will resonate throughout the interconnected system which is our shared world. The voices of individual people raised together are needed to encourage world leaders to work together and to help us create a more hopeful future for everyone.

My Personal Perspective on Progress and Success

Success is attained by the steady achievement of meaningful goals, and for me the goals are as follows:
1. Working together with global partners to create a kinder, fairer, world.
2. Supporting stress-free lifelong learning.
3. Advancing democracy by sharing success.
4. Aiming for peace and plenty for everyone.
5. Leaving the world a better place.

Expressed as a *Creative Action Plan* it looks like this:

My intention is to work with others to create a kinder, fairer world, and to leave the world a better place. I will succeed in this by:

1. Promoting effective and enjoyable *Creative Lifelong Learning* for everyone by sharing what I have learned in over forty years of helping people of all ages to progress successfully towards their goals.
2. Developing the *Creative Action Planning Process* and inviting people to form partnerships to create a kinder, fairer and more sustainable world.
3. Writing the *Creative Learning Series* to encourage people throughout the world to think carefully about how they can help to make the world a better place.

I hope that you find some inspiration and ideas in the *Creative Learning Series*. If you have, I have succeeded. If you help one person to live a better life, you help the whole world. Every good deed is potentially gifted forward, and the Creative Energy in the world is increased. I wish you every success in your life going forward, and encourage you to share your gifts freely.

About the Author

Ann Miller is a Scottish-Canadian Creative Lifelong Learning Specialist, author of *The Creative Learning Series*.

https://www.amazon.com/author/creativelearningseries